THE SINGLE PARENT'S SURVIVAL GUIDE

THE SINGLE PARENT'S SURVIVAL GUIDE

Managing Life's Challenges Alone

AVERY NIGHTINGALE

Creative Quill Press

CONTENTS

1	Introduction	1
2	Financial Management	3
3	Time Management	7
4	Emotional Well-being	11
5	Parenting Strategies	15
6	Building a Support Network	19
7	Maintaining a Healthy Lifestyle	23
8	Navigating Co-Parenting	27
9	Building Resilience	31
10	Creating a Supportive Home Environment	36
11	Self-Development and Growth	41

Copyright © 2024 by Avery Nightingale

All rights reserved. No part of this book may be reproduced in any manner whatsoever without written permission except in the case of brief quotations embodied in critical articles and reviews.

First Printing, 2024

CHAPTER 1

Introduction

An estimated 500,000 children are being raised by their grandparents. As a single parent, you need to understand that you are not alone. You are now welcome to the largest windows of communications through the myriad of support that's available. Alone, you only have two hands to manage the many faces of single parenthood, but with all this help, you have so many other hands to balance out the negatives so you can turn the lives of you and your children into something positive and constructive. In this book, you will read the "down Home" no-nonsense approach to life's cycles, laugh with some of the humorous moments, and, of course, experience a tug or two in the heart as we both recall the joy of parenthood.

Today, the number of single parent homes is on the rise, and it has fast become the new "nuclear family" of our society. Most of it has been due to changes in society and its accepted norms, and also in part to the fact that there are many more opportunities for women to be self-sufficient in society today. In 1999, there were an estimated 13.4 million single parents in the United States, and an overwhelming majority of them were single mothers. Between 1970 and 2000, the number of households with children under 18 years of age headed by a single mother nearly doubled, increasing from 3.4 million to 6.6 million, while the number of households headed by single fathers increased from more than 393,000 to more than 1.7 million.

CHAPTER 2

Financial Management

Create and keep a budget: Creating a budget is an essential task for anyone despite; remain consistent to the budget is the eventually the toughest thing. Get a reasonable idea for fitting monthly expenses into the financial statements. Breakdowns of the consumptions are not often the hindrance of this task. It is the unrealistic approach biting off a non-affordable plan prior to you begin. Compliance to a budget is exactly equivalent to self-discipline. The capability to shape desires oftentimes outstrips the financial ability to support them. Monetary self-discipline stakes control on these impulses. With practice, financial discipline can slowly transform into a pattern. Once the budget is put into use the hassle to maintain is practically gone. Every new cost should be operated by the judgment of merit to remain fitting to the financial statements. If the purchase fulfills that merit it should fall within the financial plan.

Evaluating the income: Look more at the net income versus the overall income. Begin by figuring the disposable income to guarantee all the bills are paid. This involves looking collectively at all of the month-to-month expenses. Cancel and lessen what is possible such as your cable bill or congregate expenses akin to carpooling or group tutoring. You should always examine your assets. Look for extra inflows that survive outside the everyday profits. This could be money from a second job, money from renters, financial support and any investments. Specific shortfalls should be tackled one at a time. If cash is needed, figure out how much cash is required. Next labor to complete the need through sales, loans or just basic belt cutting with the slack that has been made.

2.1. Creating a Budget

When you are going through a significant life change, such as moving, you may consider adjusting your budget and cutting your variable expenses. For example, have you considered you could save hundreds of dollars per year by cutting your cable cord or by stopping magazine subscriptions you don't read? A large expense for many working parents is the cost of commutes. Can you find a job closer to home or work from home a few days a week? There are many things to consider. Finding a job closer to home might be a dream right now, but it could happen with a plan and some focus on achieving a lifestyle that supports your main goal. I found it helpful to ask myself if spending my money on certain items would align with my goals. This usually helped me avoid spending money frivolously. Do your research. You might be surprised at how you can save.

Creating a budget doesn't have to be a scary endeavor. It is simply a plan that helps you live within your means, and financial stability looks different for everyone. Hopefully, you have put together your budget by considering both your fixed (need to pay) expenses and your variable (want to pay) expenses. Your budget also needs to take into account any child support and/or alimony (maintenance) that will help you meet your children's needs. Remember to include monthly savings in your budget. Your goal should be to save about 10–15 percent of your income every month either for a rainy day or for financial goals such as college, retirement, an emergency fund, or a car repair fund.

2.2. Saving Strategies

Many a single parent has realized that couponing can yield some extraordinary savings. It is actually a pretty addictive activity, and as an increasing number of these resources go digital, Sunday's newspaper supplement does not pack the punch it did in years past. More money-saving strategies extend beyond purchasing store-brand items or buying in bulk. Internet aggregator sites are repositories for coupon codes. Establish a constant control center to communicate with your father, monitor the news, discover buying occasions, and act as a depository for deals. Choose a product comparison to your favorite grocery item and get into the habit of checking it out before you shop. For example, if you are purchasing an essential kitchen product, will allow you to make a comparative analysis of prices.

Parenting, per se, has always been a challenge, and balancing family-related expenses against earnings significantly complicates matters. However, with the economic downturn, everyone seems to have been strained for finances, regardless of marital status, further impeding a single parent's ability to make ends meet. Be sure to survey your options; you simply cannot have everything or do everything. Make some concessions regarding some of your desires, weigh your various alternatives to reach an informed conclusion. As your children are not married to receiving all that you would want for them, they will be able to rationalize that you make a concerted effort to provide them with a comfortable life, and this experience can serve as a teaching moment in responsible decision-making.

2.3. Managing Debt

Although it's a big deal thinking about our existing bills, it still needs to be faced sooner or later. There is no benefit from staying away from it. Ignoring and avoiding payment will only generate a "snowball". A small debt will become big and may take control of our financial lives. The lack of decisiveness will make matters worse. Once caught in the debt tangle, the matter needs to be addressed before it's too late. Being decisive when things happen is the first step to building our self-esteem and mental control. Contemplating is the first step to finance management. With one thought, we are aware that we need to make the right decision and if we do it properly, we will be able to determine our lives.

Debt can once again cause feelings of failure due to not being able to provide for your family. Be suspicious of yourself and think about what you really want. Create a party plan, realistic amounts of money and time to pay off debt. The strategies needed to eliminate debt are there, but you must be ready to execute them. Debt is a necessary means today. It is used for the acquisition of goods for consumption and savings for the future. Rarely do we find a family that is living without debt. The presence of debt also has a tendency. If managed properly, debt can contribute to the improvement of a family's lifestyle, but if handled carelessly, it can undermine a family's well-being.

CHAPTER 3

Time Management

I always try to finish most of the important housework on a Sunday. My weekly menu is usually planned on the same night. A weekly plan or scheduler will help us put things into perspective. So that when you are having those moments of suddenly wondering "have you done this," "have you done that," you can refer to the timely schedule and do whatever is necessary. I usually follow my scheduler like a log, and it has been working well for me. Without a weekly schedule, more often than not, something would be neglected. I have no time to watch a movie at home, etc. I tend to appreciate peacefulness at home, sleeping, and spend the weekend going out with my child. But that depends on your schedule and how you'd like to spend it.

Single parent families are becoming more common now. It becomes a big concern to many, thinking about how and what life is going to be like being a single parent. As a single parent, time management is very important. A regular parenting plan usually will not be valid anymore. Usually, from the word go, every single parent will have this thought: "I can get my child to do homework, then at the same time clean the house, or maybe I can cook for my child while trying to split my time between concerns, both personal and professional." Even when your child is at school, you still can't manage to finish all your house chores. A combination of work, house chores, and single parenting responsibilities are very demanding. Here are a few tips to lower your stress level when you have only 24 hours every day.

3.1. Prioritizing Tasks

2. Get it out of your head. I'm a big one for writing things down. That's not to say I ever remember to read the lists, mind you: they're more for comfort to show me that I must be getting something done because there's a list and it's written by yours truly. Some people, if they didn't write it down, certainly won't remember it, but once items are outside your head, you might find you've got more room there, and more patience to corral what's left inside your noggin into a more behaved manner.

1. Find a system that works for you. Many people swear by to-do lists, like writer Mennen Tonnell, whose successful blog about to-do lists is called, what else? "What's my next?" Sometimes the list is long, other times the more specific "inner task list" that Tonnell uses is broken into project lists with a wider scope. Soccer mom guru Cyndi Haynes recommends two lists systematically developed with the help of her son. As having an eight-year-old muse might not be on everyone's list of resources, my advice is to read widely and experiment with systems to discover the best one for you.

As a single parent, you need to learn to get very good at organizing and setting the order of importance to your priorities. I'm terrible at it. At any given time, I will have fifty-seven things on the go, and I struggle daily with trying to decide which ones should be allowed into my stressful world. I used to have a daily nervous breakdown until I realized that this wasn't conducive to getting things done (shocking, I know). If you're better at multitasking than I, bully for you. Here are some tricks to help both of us prioritize our daily lives.

3.2. Setting Realistic Goals

Therefore, to ensure success and set realistic goals for yourself and for your children, single parents must adhere to the fable of the man with a goose that laid golden eggs. In this fable, a poor man comes upon a goose that laid golden eggs. The man believes that if he holds on to the goose he will become very rich. So each day, he takes an egg and then another and another until the goose lays no more eggs. That is the ending of the clear emphasis on moderation. As you move forward in life, you must be careful not to get overextended. Putting in too many extra work hours or running to every event that your children are involved in can lead to dissatisfaction in you and can confuse your children. It also disallows your children from learning how to fend on their own.

First of all, a single parent must be realistic about their own capabilities. You are only one person and you can only do so many things. Setting yourself up for failure does nothing but lower your self-confidence level and that is not good for anyone. A single parent who is trying to hold down a full-time job, manage a household, and take care of the extracurricular activities of children needs to be a superhero in their own mind. It is not humanly possible to accomplish everything, no matter how hard you try.

If you are like most single parents, you often feel like you are trying to get everything done and everything that happens that you cannot control is another brick in the wall. It is impossible to get everything done and be everything to everyone. The situation can eat at the fiber of your spirit and throw your well-intended outlook on life into a spiral. The problem for many single parents is that they do not plan and set expectations for themselves and for their children. Life can be very complicated and as a single parent, life can be even more complicated. Planning and managing are difficult tasks, but to succeed in life as a single parent, they must be done.

3.3. Effective Scheduling

And what about sudden changes in the schedule that often appear with a child? Similarly here, one should approach these problems with routines. If you have a rhythm, you can adhere to that rhythm even if a playdate or friends from the same age group come over. All in all, when combining job, parenthood, and free time, time management is essential. Some tasks can be performed rather quickly, other actions need more time, which not only has to be taken into consideration when planning but also when fulfilling the time plan. Determined and motivated mothers who wish to combine job and family will also be successful.

You should make a plan for every single day because it's the only way you will get things done. In your plan, you should consider everything: the time you get up, make the beds, breakfast, your breaks, even every walk you take with your kid. Only with such a plan will you be able to make enough time for each task and create a routine. By achieving this, working single mothers can engage in parenthood, work, and a social life. So, if some things are not accomplished on that day, it is okay. Each day is a new beginning. Such a plan may seem hard to carry out at the beginning, but if you try and set limits, for instance, eating should not last more than half an hour, it gets easier quickly.

CHAPTER 4

Emotional Well-being

The stronger you are, the better equipped you will be to deal with the inevitable, and the more you can resist predicting insidious consequences. Do not let the negative anticipations become a self-fulfilling prophecy. The stronger and more complete you are, then as your children reach adulthood, they, in many circumstances, will follow the life's pattern of their parents. A well-thought-out parenting plan is not only a good way to manage your child's time but also to be able to set an example of how to build healthy relationships outside the family structure down the line.

It is essential for a single-parent family to fall into a continuing pattern of good emotional health and positive self-esteem, provided the parent sets a pattern for managing their personal life, ensuring the ability to have gratifying relationships with others. When one tends to be physically, spiritually, and emotionally whole, a negative personal experience with a marital partner can be less likely to adversely affect one's personal relationships in the future. Children who are reared in a healthy family unit are also likely to emulate this type of emotional well-being, preparing children to lead healthy adult relationships through good life experiences demonstrated by both their divorced single parents.

4.1. Self-Care Practices

First of all, single mothers need to understand that it is their responsibility to claim time for themselves and to take care of themselves. They need to understand that if they don't take time for themselves, they may become restless, ill or angry. They may become tired and crabby. They may not be around for their children as long as they could be had they taken better care of themselves. If they don't regularly get a chance to unwind, to re-prioritize, re-group...they won't be the mother or person they would like to be. The mother at her best is worth the time for self-care. Once understood, self-care can and will become a priority for single mothers. Self-care will not bring instant change to anyone's life, but it will create the intent to be more mindful of our thoughts and actions involving our own care. There is a difference between "selfishness" and the practice of good self-care.

1. If asked, most professional experts would probably say the same thing. Taking care of oneself is the single most important action we can do to take care of others. Because of the hurried pace that mothers (and single parents) hold today, the basic ways in which to take care of oneself are often overlooked, forgotten or misunderstood. Single mothers cannot give to their children or others what they do not have themselves. When mothers live healthy, balanced lives and model positive self-care, their children benefit exponentially. There's no way around it - taking time for yourself is not indulgence, it's not a selfish act, and it is not wasteful. On the contrary, needing to be constantly needed is an exhausting way to live.

4.2. Seeking Support

Many people also suggest that it can be very helpful to establish periodic events for other women facing the same situation in our local community, such as birth preparation courses, postpartum groups, and so on. It may seem difficult to find other single mothers, but there are many, we just have to find them. So, we can share support, advice, time, and also share the kids between us from time to time, in order to have free time without spending a fortune. There are other women in your same area, do not be so difficult to find them. We are many and we are everywhere. No one will know who you are if you are the one to stimulate and encourage the organization of some group activities. How can you say whether a mother is single or not? She can pretend to encourage you, by doing a few searches on the web, by visiting mothers and babies groups, etc. When you feel free, you will find a lot of positive energy that will push you to continue in this direction. You will also be a source of inspiration for someone else, even if it seems hard to you, regardless of the point your life is currently at. Let's be cooperative with each other, whenever possible.

Some single parents are self-sufficient and proud of it. Others, while self-sufficient, have put their needs, hobbies, and social lives aside and "delegate everything to themselves." According to many single moms, one of the best ways of getting support is to look for the right community. Many people around you can actually help you. It is only about having access to them. Are we willing to show our vulnerability? Talking about loneliness, sexual life, economic problems in social media is a good way to start. It is a way of communicating valuable information consciously, without showing embarrassment that we are alone. It's the best way I know to ask for support without really "asking for it." Talking about others and also giving what we receive, without reservation, with no strings attached, on the same level. Either they are hard cash or clear information, let's consider that everything we receive is earned. And let's try, in our turn, to help those who are in the same position we were, or even those who are a step or two behind us. Knowledge is power.

4.3. Coping with Stress

There are many things in daily life we try to buy in bulk to save money. However, with the ones that are not used frequently, we are likely to have to throw out a large amount. Besides, we are occupied with large plastic containers that have to be stored. I no longer purchase traces of daily products if I don't use them frequently. I use them enough when I need them and don't use them altogether. This allows me time to contemplate whether to buy them again. For all things, normally three quarters are the unseen remainder. If there are 10 q-tips left, that means 25 q-tips when they are new. Naturally, when there are 15 of something left when I see 10, the intact new remainders to multiply are 30% more. The savings might not be very appreciable, but this is a doubly pleasing tidbit if we are able to save with the feeling that we are not living wastefully.

Everyone has his or her own troubles. There are plenty of things that I cannot see beyond what is in front of me, myself desiring to see to a child's physical and mental health, nurturing worries about the opposition, financial troubles never disappearing. However, sometimes such troublesome days are quite rewarding. When my daughter cured the cold and cough that she had for a month with acupuncture massage, she was so pretty as she went back to school looking lively. The opponents remaining quiet is rewarding. It is difficult to make the accounts balance with the loan and the rare pay cheque. I can't afford the basics while they take time to pass, then when we are not expecting it, the large corner of our cake is eaten by a large company. The song that says "Pennywise and pound foolish" is right. I try to save money on futile things and buy it, then notice tomorrow that we are lacking the things we really need. I will pray.

The biggest stress for single parents is just getting up in the morning and fulfilling their duties. As an alone parent, I can't ask anybody to give the infant medicine or to hold the baby while I change his diaper and cook dinner. Moreover, what hurts the most is that when I hold the baby the entire day, my arms and back become tired. At such times, I am extremely tired both physically and mentally. To pull myself together, I depend on my great treasures, my kids. When we run out of energy, we play. Even during the busy hours of task finishing, to make time to laugh together means so much. Even a moment of laughter refreshes me. When things reach a really bad stage, I ask for help. There are persons who will help without refusal. When I ask for help, I tell them clearly how to help me. Self-help is very important.

CHAPTER 5

Parenting Strategies

3) Schedule time for yourself. Parenting can quickly begin to take over your life. It becomes a full-time job, and not just the job you do to pay your bills. No other aspect of life demands as much time and effort or has a greater impact. For this reason, make an effort to carve out time in your schedule for self-care. Make whatever adjustments are necessary to make sure you're devoting some time to yourself on a regular basis. Whether you leave your kids with your former partner on certain weekends or you schedule an occasional in-home sitter, make it happen.

2) Instill help. Single parents often ask their children to help with chores and errands. This encourages their children to learn new skills and become more responsible. But while all kids need to learn how to step up to the plate, in families with one parent, this help often means the child is playing a greater role in the family dynamic than would typically be the case. This isn't a bad thing, but they also require some control. Find the balance between encouraging help and reliance without allowing the child to become totally responsible for the household.

1. Provide structure and discipline. Children thrive on routine. Stick to a regular schedule - this sense of security is especially crucial for young children. Maintain family rituals such as regular mealtimes and set bedtimes. For a single parent, parenting provides

the structure. Many single parents report that their child's needs help them to focus on what's important. Discipline your children when necessary. By knowing what to expect, children are provided with a sense of boundaries and limits that are crucial to managing behavior.

5.1. Establishing Routines

Discussion with your child(ren) begging for solutions, wisdom from an expert, suggestions found online, and with classes in local institutions help to fine-tune routines or create new ones. Single parenting creates a lifestyle that isn't a choice. Discern this is what needs to happen to maximize the promise of a child's potential. Never be satisfied to just stay surviving day by day since we personally are the most influential thing in a child's life. If the most prominent influence doesn't provide the structure and direction that lead to surrounding with people that create the windows of opportunity, there will be much more difficulty in facing poverty, whether it is related to education and what career opportunities that flow from it for the children long term or just the immediate of keeping food on the table and a roof over every head. In addition, we are signaling the mold that moving away from poverty is the common goal. Therefore, youth will likely value a universally accepted scoreboard within their peer group, possibly replacing the one of living to an adult in warmth and under the watch of someone elsewhere.

Routines provide the necessary structure and predictability that children crave. Establish daily routines for mealtimes, getting up and going to bed, homework, screen time, and chore time. When children don't follow through with their responsibilities, don't get sucked into doing it all: "Let natural consequences occur because they truly are the most valuable teachers in our kids' lives for so many things." Your child's success will depend on your structure. The more intact providing structure the parent can do, the better the outcomes will be for your child. When you know what is expected and are able to physically manage the time to do what's expected, the flow of the morning, the meal schedule, and chore time will create a rhythmic dance that has confidence available to be inside of during the unexpected – when those things hit. Your day is owned. Because routines can always use fine-tuning, ask if there are more effective ways to do the everyday necessities making up our days. How can we make constructive the time in the car from school to soccer practice? How should homework be handled better? When alone, choose things that can be stopped or paused: routines you can say "pretend I do not have kids" to create the ability to do what absolutely needs to be done.

5.2. Discipline Techniques

But 69 percent of the young survey respondents also believe that parents aren't strict enough. Their complaint? They feel strict parents are better at keeping children on the straight and narrow, ultimately leading them to greater confidence and the ability to make more important decisions once they become adults. The parents of earlier generations also had stories to tell; they had family values and they adopted discipline techniques that eventually led to independent and respectful adults. It is our responsibility as today's parents to adapt and modify these principles and techniques as appropriate. As parents, we need to analyze recent changes in our society and the significant change in social structures, and the related challenges for us and, most importantly, our children. With this knowledge, we should be able to determine appropriate ways to guide and lead our children in the right direction.

According to the Discovery Report, released in February 2004 by the British-based Future Foundation, a significant majority of Canadians aged 16 to 24 are in agreement that today's parents are more "liberal" in terms of discipline than were their own parents. The Discovery Report, which is part of an ongoing survey focusing on people in the age group called Generation Y or Echo Boomers, showed that only 11 percent of those surveyed say today's parents are strict disciplinarians. What's more, a considerable majority of Generation Y people say it is alright for kids to "talk back" to their parents. According to the Discovery Report, a full 76 percent of those surveyed agree that it's okay for young people to talk back if they have been respectful.

5.3. Balancing Work and Parenting

Women who are single parents have created a reasonably ordered life, integrating families, work, and friends. Possibly juggling it all at a cost that no one can really afford. Unfortunately, there are important aspects of life that many of us short-change. Women have written marvelously and works that have identified the sources of unsatisfied dreams, dreams that are cast aside or, alternatively perhaps, never created in the quest of achieving supercare status. A better, more balanced hierarchy is needed but what that structure looks like is unfamiliar, unvisited territory. Napoleon Hill in his book, Think and Grow Rich, states that few of us have a finite pursuit. Fewer of us achieve the things we want before it is too late to enjoy their benefits.

Life often feels like a juggling act. There are so many balls to keep in the air, and if we drop one, we experience regret. Sometimes, life feels like it's about nothing but a series of near-misses. Many parents - single or not - struggle with how to create what they consider to be the right balance between work and family. However, most of us achieve some sort of balance. Whether your dollars are stretched or not, a life without the twinkle of children's voices or the promise of a day yet to come puts the intricacies of work and jobs into perspective. There are mental health dangers in not having enough autonomy within a job, but the presence of small humans often provides a profound reason to "suffer fools gladly" and do things differently than you would do for your own basic needs alone. Going to work is often the respite for a single parent. Although often, the disaster of mismatched socks, failed breakfasts, and nerves created by non-matching socks can cloud the knowledge that your sane hours sitting in meetings "away from it all" actually make the "whole" possible.

CHAPTER 6

Building a Support Network

Gather regularly with your single parent community. You cannot talk with married friends and expect them to have anything to offer but the most superficial advice. If you are to reduce the level of feelings of powerlessness that will consume your life, you need to find people who are also being affected by this.

Find groups that provide other single parents with adult companionship. One of the main reasons a single parent has to be vigilant as far as their mental health and energy is loneliness. Each month, go out at least once, getting yourself a really good break in the process. This should cost about 100 dollars, provided you do it on the cheap. Allow your single parent friends the opportunity of providing this service or go out and enjoy time to yourself if you can afford it.

Have your therapist provide counseling to your children while you meet other parents who are going through the same thing. Many single parents drop the ball on this but pursuing enjoyable activities in the right way can be literally life-saving. Research supports the fact that good friends are the best path to happiness and longevity.

Start building these relationships by showing up early for school events, sports events, or finding a family at church that you really admire. Take your time making this happen but remember that it is vitally important.

Create relationships with other families that you enjoy hanging out with. These parents and their children can help you by providing an example of a family unit that works, which is a great practical teaching tool, as well as friends that become a part of your life.

You cannot go it alone. There are many other single parents out there who are struggling mightily just to keep their heads above water. The fact is, you cannot survive by yourself. You need a support network. You must actively go out and try to create that network. Some of the following suggestions are also encouraged as a way of doing that.

6.1. Connecting with Other Single Parents

Conversing with other single mothers also provides one with the unique perspective to view one's family in a different light. Many single mothers reported feeling as though they have had to grow up too quickly or that they were too young to have children as they did, or further, that no one else could understand their experience as a teen mother. However, as they compared experiences, they outgrew those feelings of isolation and self-pity and began to view and understand their family in a more positive light. These received benefits, needs, and general support from other single mothers result in the development of homophily and, ultimately, the motivated resources of support as rewards.

Research indicates that the experience of single motherhood is not an isolated one, but rather a shared experience among an increasing number of U.S. households. It is worth noting, however, that not all single mothers necessarily contribute to or even create this supportive network. In Chapter 2, I describe single mothers' living arrangements. Yet, single mothers often maintain meaningful relationships with friends, family, and fellow single mothers. For example, they maintain different types of living arrangements, which help them to avoid feelings of isolation. And this is especially needed when participating in the most popular form of social connection, which is sharing children's needs and experiences with other single mothers. Many sample respondents described the meaningful support that talking to other single mothers provides. One respondent described that connecting with other single mothers helped to relieve feelings of loneliness and helped her to cope with the challenges and stresses of family life.

6.2. Utilizing Community Resources

Consider your specific situation. What are your strengths, talents, and things you enjoy? Are you truly content with being a stay-home parent? Do you wish you didn't have to work as many hours? What are your job opportunities? Could you possibly work at home? What are your education goals? Have you considered co-housing, or shared living situations? Maybe you're an outstanding cleaner and could barter child care for housecleaning services once each week. Maybe you are an animal lover and can manage pet sitting for evenings and weekends out in trade for pet sitting when you work or vacation. Remember to consider your children. They also will be better off with more positive and quality time. I believe life is an experiment. You don't know how it will turn out until you try it!

Through surveying my single-mom friends' communities, I found a more common thread in our needs and resources. The following is a list of community resources which you should check on availability in your area: babysitting co-ops, single-parent support groups, car pools, parent aides, public library, church support, parent-child groups, financial counseling, food co-ops, low-cost reduced care programs, clothing exchanges, car clubs, energy assistance programs, second-hand stores, utilities programs, discount purchasing programs, community services, crisis intervention services, health and welfare, discount transportation programs, public school programs, public hospital and health clinics, free dental clinic and low-cost reduced care programs. Not all are specific to single parents, but single parents have specific needs and sometimes generic community resources won't meet those needs as well as a specific resource would. Don't be afraid to ask a new friend or someone who's been in the community longer. You will be very pleasantly surprised by how generous people can be. (On the other hand, remember not to take advantage of your resources, or the resource loses its purpose.)

6.3. Engaging in Support Groups

Restrict the amount of time you spend with your single status and, in general, view yourself first as a parent, an individual deserving of love, respect, and tolerance. Encourage your children to volunteer at youth centers, with other single parent families, with senior citizens, and within other groups that welcome their participation. Viability for future life challenges is readily acquired by participation in such activities. Young children benefit from giving unselfishly of themselves and families can bond together in such giving activities. Apart from building a stronger bond in your family unit, emphasizing such positive activities in the life of a child diverts his interest in associating with unfavorable characters.

Adopt the role of leader and/or active participant in local support groups geared toward the circumstances surrounding your life as a single parent. In an attempt to ensure that such support groups have the best positive influence on your life, make a conscious effort to avoid groups that involve difficult people or support groups which propagate self-pity. This particular aspect is important because surrounding yourself with individuals who are full of self-pity may serve to aggravate the stressors associated with single parenting. Engaging in such activities can undeniably foster negative tendencies. Instead, seek out positive parents willing to provide help and moral support to you and your family, thereby learning from them highly effective coping strategies.

CHAPTER 7

Maintaining a Healthy Lifestyle

Exercise: Life is increasingly demanding and impairs the time required for traditional training. Exceptional planning and time management talents also provide great physical activity opportunities by daily routes. During work hours, biographies, and group moments, consider various forms of physical activity. Encourage meetings, walking meetings, or staggered breaks. Make sure you are dressed for a workout that includes regular activities. Regular activities offer the additional benefit of strengthening family connections, which is especially important for the single parent family! Activities of the family provide memorable fun and relationship building possibilities, and establish lifelong habits. Aerobic activities like cycling, swimming, walking, or step are important for heart health and social health as they incorporate close friends and loved ones. Consider strength training and yoga exercises to enhance both excellent body strength and mental clarity: excellent for a healthy life.

Healthy Eating: Always make time to eat regular, nutritious meals by buying a variety of whole traditional foods, such as fresh fruit, and frozen vegetables. Read labels and avoid anything with excessive preservatives, additives, or trans fats. Avoid or limit caffeine, alcohol, and tobacco, as well as sugar and fatty foods. While easy-to-prepare meals and fast snacks are always in stock, make full use of the power of a well-stocked kitchen. Healthy meal preparation strategies are just as healthy and delicious as a delightful 'fast' setup or order in. Attempt to prepare in advance and eat together as a family. Regular meals are basic, healthy communication habits! This makes it easier to decide what you are interested in and definitely limits unhealthy snacks.

It's no secret that life is demanding and, at times, the urge to turn to immediate gratification saves your energy or time. Health is your and your family's most valuable asset. Maintaining a healthy lifestyle is essential for peace of mind and maintaining your poise, even during tough times. Here are three key essentials of managing healthy lifestyle habits:

7.1. Nutrition and Meal Planning

The three predictor signs that a child will develop an eating disorder in their adolescence are dieting, fear of fat and food, and low self-esteem. 56% of our children eat with both parents, and 89% of kids eat dinners with their parents. Research shows that children who do not eat dinners with their families gain 1 ½ pounds more weight than kids who eat at least three dinners with family a week. TextStyle also found that 72% of youth want to eat meals with both parents. Reducing the risks of malnutrition through living as a single parent and keeping our kids healthy can be very challenging. An important step is to help our child's communication and nutrition to increase.

Living alone with a child means one adult is often juggling all the responsibilities. This includes cooking and helping a child eat well. Developing a nutrition philosophy is an important step to give peace and security when feeding our children. My child was diagnosed with a gluten/wheat allergy several years ago. At our parent-child nutrition sessions, we take the time to eat more meals and snacks together to increase our ability to easily communicate about nutrition. The struggle facing single parents is often communication/language challenges, especially in child nutrition. It is important that we all learn to comfortably talk about nutrition at all ages with everyone.

7.2. Fitness and Exercise

7.2. Fitness and Exercise: This weekend, I went for a good tramp around my favourite part of the Port Hills near my home - I should be doing that every morning, but the problem is the same: time - where do I get it? For when? I know the rewards are brilliant - getting out into the fresh air, into the changing surroundings, the company of myself, feeling the life of nature, etc. - the same reasons I give when I talk to friends about getting back to yoga - but I think I've missed the point of the line "But where do I get the time?" If it was a priority, then I would schedule it in and work everything else around that. Time is then more available, and most likely, the things I do now (idle mostly) will have to be compressed into the time I allow myself to build in fitness work - hence I will do less of the things I know are non-priority stuff.

Challenges: Doing too much: I know it's tempting to 'do it all', but be careful not to 'overdo' doing it all. Everything looks like a priority when you are a solopreneur, capable and driven, but other things suffer as a result. One of the first things I've allowed myself to drop when things got really busy was me. I let go of exercise, time for myself, time for friends, etc. I recently took up swimming and it felt really good, but since Archie's ear operation, I've dropped that again. Every time I look at my swimsuit and shake my head, feeling the weight of those extra kilos dragging out my droopy swim fabric, I wonder why I don't simply schedule time for it - it is only 20 minutes, and I'm sure Archie will survive in the playpen for that time.

7.3. Sleep and Rest

It gives you the ability to awaken ready to face the day in a way that reflects your dreams and ambitions. Independent, thoughtful planning frees your mental faculties to be influential in an infinite number of possibilities that unfold with the dawn. Remember that the only constant in life is change. By envisioning and preparing for the day to come, you begin to eliminate the disruptions to your serenity that you might encounter. Letting yourself be fully conscious of the calming peace that envelops you each night will help you to sleep soundly. With a minimum of six hours of sleep, preferably eight, you allow yourself to benefit from the hours of darkness that lull you gently.

Establishing sleep routines is important for your child's development. Just as children benefit from a regular bedtime, grown-ups find it helpful to follow a regular relaxation schedule and bedtime patterns. Often a quiet cup of chamomile tea, a hot bath, reading inspirational literature, or a few minutes of loving meditation before you tuck yourself in will help you move peacefully into sleep. As you rest, picture the events in the coming day as you wish them to unfold. As you conclude your time of reflection, bless the day that has ended with appreciation, and then bless the day that is about to begin with beautiful expectations and perfect planning.

CHAPTER 8

Navigating Co-Parenting

Adulting is a relatively new term, but in fact it's a philosophy that's been around for more than 30 years. We know it's important to take action – finish school, seek work, pay bills, have fun, etc. Today, I'm the mother of two boys and a girl who work hard, go to school every day, and treat everyone they meet with respect. Fortunately, they take their parenting goals responsibly. However, if you look at their father and me, you wouldn't think we were doing well. In the eyes of co-parenting, we must be adolescents. Our communication is, at best, weak, and at worst, futile. I find that we often assume that our children will eat us and that they will pick up the remains long after it decays. From experience, we know that perpetual bitterness damages children. However, you – and I – must make an effort. In this area, it is worth our time and effort. To be a better person, a better parent, and a better friend, the effort applies. After all, success will not come overnight when successfully co-fit parenting. However, it's worth it when our children reach their goal and reach their potential, receiving certificates from the parent poster.

You have gone through the single parent challenges – the strain of supporting your children alone, juggling their schedules, and managing household tasks without a partner's support. Now there's a new hurdle – working with a spouse who's no longer a spouse. Co-parenting amicably sounds like an obvious choice, but it's not an easy one, particularly in the wake of a strained relationship. But if implemented, it can be a great success. Parenting as a team allows both of you to be active participants in your children's lives. Raising boys without a male role model and girls without a female is no small feat. With this in mind, your child's best interest must be at stake. Despite the many obstacles, for the sake of our children, we must make every effort to work comfortably with our co-parent.

8.1. Effective Communication

In order to communicate openly and confidently, how the parent encourages the family to demonstrate emotional literacy, provide a sense of unity and understanding, to discuss the open dialogue, and commitment to the family members in the event of uncertainty. Children and adolescents will greatly contribute to the household if family values are fulfilled. Disagreements, disputes, contradictions, and difficulties occur when family values are disrespect. It's important to have a solid lifestyle for the family. This makes it easier for both parents and children as well.

Aim to avoid the words "pain," "suffer," "sad," and "sad." If kids whine too much and complain about issues in their lives they will eventually withdraw you. The problems of their small children need to be treated equally easily. Place yourself in the shoes of your child to better understand the issue. Treat it as equally in their mind. Develop a judgement to figure out what they've done so far in their minds. In the meantime, ask your child for more detail.

Parent-child communication can be practiced through role play, asking painless questions with easy answers, using questions from round as starters, and guiding the conversation. Whether it is for parental social level, family level, practical level, or personal level, being proficient encourages good communication. The family will be generally happy with good communication. Parental social level can be helped as well, if they know they are ready and can talk to children and teenagers. Interview questions can be role-played to guide children. It is also an excellent guide to speak with children. Casual questions can be used, 'yes' or 'no' focused, round questions can be difficult. Personal questions are probably the most effective when questions encourage your children's thought.

8.2. Coordinating Schedules

People become single parents for many reasons: the death of a spouse, a marriage breakup, or a divorce, out-of-wedlock pregnancies, which is becoming more and more common, and the end of a relationship. Parenting alone can be difficult, and you make many sacrifices – especially on your personal time, responsibilities, and achievements. This does not mean you cannot raise a dysfunctional family. Creating a support system is vital to surviving and raising a family alone. Depending on your unique situation, adopting new rules, breaking some traditional old folks' habits will go a long way for the family. You have to remember that you are transitioning from a partner to a single parent, and all partners' short-term and long-term goals become yours. Partners come together with their individual needs and individual goal settings. You both merge to become a team of united common goals, yet you both also have individual goals that may sometimes in the normal course of life be overlooked, thereby fostering discord.

In two-parent families, the children often see that both parents are pulling together in their efforts - each parent has the responsibility for both his/her needs and his/her own, as well as the needs of the family. In single-parent families, the family by definition is personalized and individualized around the one caretaker. The children almost always have developed relationships with both their parents, and that is something both of them can build on when deciding on the logistics of coordinating time and managing child rearing efforts for their own children.

8.3. Resolving Conflict

But still, they do help, if even in small ways. They help when they say something that really was lying in the back of your mind all the time; when they ask if you're OK without them even realizing what they did; when they take it upon themselves to research something; when they play with their siblings without being asked; when they point out that working out might be a good idea. It's those unplanned moments that are the most touching, teaching you that children don't always need an adult around to take care of things. Good things can even happen when mom/dad isn't at her/his best and they're the only adult around, highlighting that maybe they are learning to take care of themselves. When you step back from whatever it is that's overwhelming, asking if maybe you're not helping them more this way. After all, most of the time the few bright spots that light your day are a result of them being kids, not through any help you're receiving.

No matter how focused you are on creating an adult partnership with your child, there's no getting around the fact that kids just aren't equipped to take care of your emotional or practical support needs. This is generally the last thing they're thinking of or can be expected to do. And they shouldn't. They should be left to play with the neighbor kids, do their homework, talk with you about their day at school, help out around the house, or do the 500 other things kids need to grow up healthy and happy. And having been raised in single parent households doesn't mean that the one thing they should do in life is take care of their parent. That just isn't the way to nurture a healthy and loving relationship with your child.

CHAPTER 9

Building Resilience

Moving from the stage of surviving to thriving isn't easy, but the following strategies offered by Jan Bruce, co-founder of meQuilibrium, can help you build your reserves of resilience so you have the strength and brainpower to meet adversity head-on. By managing our thinking, emotions, and reactions, we can approach challenges with confidence. We can engage in the face of adversity and channel the energy of that experience in the direction of what's paramount to us; we can thrive. First, choose optimism and intentionally reframe the situation. Don't presume the worst. Remember an example from the past when something positive came from a difficult time. Then, cultivate a strong social network. It's important to cultivate the right relationships and recognize how to amplify your happiness around the right people. Consider writing down your goals and experiences. Reflect and potentially gain perspective on your feelings and patterns, and capture life in a way that makes it more meaningful. Don't deny your feelings – respect and allow the time needed to grieve the loss or process – then reframe. Evaluate the situation and be grateful for and become thankful for the experiences that refine your life. Building your own resilience is key to raising happy, healthy, confident children as well as essential to your development, your mental health, happiness, and well-being – especially in times of stress and adversity and when managing life as a single parent.

Finding healthy ways to cope and get through a crisis or difficult time is hard, no matter who you are. Life can be extremely overwhelming and lonely sometimes, and we all know that solitary existence can magnify and prolong the impact of stress and adversity. There's a famous quote often credited to Charles Darwin: "It is not the strongest of the species that survive, but the one most responsive to change." The same can be said about those who thrive in the face of adversity. We all know that resilience – that ability to turn adversity into an opportunity or triumph by reprogramming our thinking – is an important key to raising happy, healthy, confident children. But it's also a part of our own self-help survival kit, necessary for our mental health, happiness, well-being, and the development of healthy relationships.

9.1. Cultivating a Positive Mindset

Instead of harboring negative thoughts like these, focus on the good things you bring to the job as a parent, how far you've come, how much stronger and wiser you are. As a single parent, you get to be the caregiver, teacher, emotional support, role model, mentor, and hero. Consider the rewards of single parenting. Consider the big picture associated with your role. Possessing a positive attitude may be the most important attribute a single parent can have. Negative attitudes are contagious and yield no benefits. By working to exude a positive attitude, you're providing an amazing example for your children who will develop their own positive mentality by watching you. Throughout everyday living, good and bad things happen. It's easy to lose focus from the good and dwell on the bad. By offering yourself forgiveness, focusing on a positive attitude, using positive self-talk, incorporating problem-solving into everyday living, and cultivating the ability to learn and grow, single parenting can and will be survived.

If you're a single parent, cultivate a positive attitude and use a lot of positive self-talk. It's easy to fall into a pattern of "I can't" or "it's too hard." You may even replay in your mind all the negative messages about single parenting. You think about people who have pitied you or have said derogatory things about single parents. You may think about people who've said you've failed or are "damaged goods" since your relationship ended. The thoughts seem to multiply and grow.

9.2. Overcoming Obstacles

In short, I neither acknowledged the depth nor accommodations said to our guests. Yet these very same guests, like the jet crash victims, are people. They have histories that give rise to all states of mind. Some may even be aware that they no longer acknowledge their personal state except as another positive or negative occurrence. These people are real people, living in situations that are far too often discarded as a phase in life that we ourselves could escape. I correct my attitude as often as possible. Our guests need more than the three basics, so we offer 15 auxiliary services. I consciously acknowledge the presence and need for flexibility elements required by our guests as often as I can. Our shelter staff members do the same, and a kind attitude is widely embraced during these interactions. To some outsiders, Intake assessments appear hurried. They may come across lightly or not serious enough to food and shelter. That's not the only result of such procedures. With the right attitude and a deep respect for their individuality, those few days spent with guests can become the refuge they need.

I discovered an interesting shift in my attitudes as I was working in the kitchen one evening. I was preparing a meal while watching the nightly news; the volume went down, and the next scenes portrayed images of a civilian jet crash site. As always in such disasters, rescue workers were combing through the rubble attempting to find survivors. That's when it occurred to me. My first thought was, "I hope they find someone." The funny part was the personal pronoun. When I thought about it, I changed from a passing observer to one having some interest in the event. It struck me as funny. Why would anyone care whether someone survived or not? We get about 400 guests a week at Good Samaritan Haven. I have done countless intakes for single-person households, ex-refugees, or a mother and children from Short-Term Family Housing. I understand how unsettling coming to shelter can be and work hard to do this with dignity for our guests. Yet I never really thought about what they would feel like while coming through the process of "emergency housing" was for them. (I do know the overwhelming gratitude that follows intake was present when I entered temporary housing. It's huge.) Most often emergency housing is seen as a temporary solution. It brings with it the expectation of hurry in finding an income and permanent housing option. This is not taking into account those other things going on in their lives, and it's really not enough.

9.3. Embracing Change

Change represents something unfamiliar, different, and new. Thus, what defines our lives isn't the changes we face, but how we accept them, what we choose to do about them, and how we react. Each of us needs to hold a powerful and passionate belief in the extraordinary transformational power of change and embrace the rapid transformation that's reshaping our world. We can't shirk it, hide from it, ignore it, curse it, tremble in fear, or call it impossible; it's here, and it's amazing. We can either sit by the sidelines and watch the world go by us, or choose to start taking an active role in creating the kind of life that moves in the direction that's right for us now. The path to our destiny is determined by the decisions we make each day, each moment, every moment. Every risk we take, every move we make, every change we face and following embrace, helps us go the extra mile and get us closer to the goal. Welcome change like you never could before, and not only build upon it, but also grow and transform from it.

It takes courage to embrace change when your heart is holding on with a fierce grip to the past. We all face difficulties in life, and when most of us do, we hold on to the idea of normalcy. This is where we are comfortable, where we understand, and where we excel. It's what we know, and letting go and embracing what's new is something that's been conditioned in us, something we've been trained to reject. We haven't embraced anything new or unfamiliar since we were children. And children see newness as exciting, surprising, and invigorating. But over time, as we become too comfortable and familiar with what we already know, it's easy to become nervous, unsure, and uncomfortable when changes arise.

CHAPTER 10

Creating a Supportive Home Environment

'Everyone is a team-mate' means that everyone helps out. You don't do everything for your kids, taking time away from all the things you need to do. They are part of the team and can enjoy the satisfaction of helping themselves. Childhood is a time of learning, and it is important for kids to learn independence from you. It may be difficult in the short-term but is tremendously beneficial to them in the long-term. Understand that the more kids cook for themselves, clean up after themselves, and take part in 'managing the house,' the more they feel part of the team effort in this enterprise - the family.

Have a 'place' for everything. Everyone, including your children (as soon as they are coordinated enough) should know where things go. You can even take pictures of objects and tape them on drawers or shelves to remind them where everything goes. Label things with words and pictures, even in the refrigerator and pantry. This creates a smooth, organized operating environment and reduces stress - everyone will know where to find and put things away. The burden of what needs to be done to manage a home can be distributed through routines and everyone taking part in community living. The downside of this - that nobody is a 'princess' or a 'prince' is actually a plus!

Keep things simple. A calm and uncluttered home is a happy home. Consider telling children that they can keep only things that fit into their rooms. This should encourage them to avoid clutter, while you also clean out. The same goes for their possessions. You want them to choose only essentials to fit with the basics you already have. Avoid TV programs or media that are clutter-filled. Choose shows, movies, and music that support your simple lifestyle. Tell children that memories and love are what make them special, not possessions, and that the environment around them should reflect this.

10.1. Establishing a Safe Space

Reiterate that you have a plan and that if something does go wrong, you will be there as soon as possible. Connection with other parents, and the child's trust that other parents will help, will also ease some fears the parent may have. Building that circle of trust goes a long way toward lower stress at home. Becoming a single parent means also becoming a single source for the child's needs. A simple breakdown in a family car must be considered. Do we have a budget for repairs? Does the repair come before a bill? Is one car sufficient if it breaks down? This makes a new single parent gig worker even more vulnerable to their means of transportation! Even simple things like a large unexpected auto expense can cause much larger financial stress and trepidation about bills and food on the table. Always considering what could go wrong is something that a single parent path very much hides from public view. The reason the world does not see the desperation of the single parent is because the single parent is consistently creating a shield of safety and security.

Now that custody arrangements are set and the single parent embarks on the adventure of raising their most precious assets, the children, finding a safe space for children is a requirement. No parent wants to picture their child alone after school with no one to talk to or play with, and time and effort is put into finding a trusted helper after school, or maybe forming a support network with other parents. One thing that the single parent must remember is that a parent's fears often transfer to their own children. "What time will you be back?" "Where will you be?" "Are you with a responsible adult?" The parents' anxiety becomes the child's anxiety. "What will I do?" "Where will I go?" "I can't reach my parent. Why aren't they answering? Have they been in an accident?" By establishing routines, select check-ins, and consistent "see you after school!" and "Welcome home!" parents can slowly ease the "horror movie coverage" tension the child may carry. Moreover, many times the parent could use the words "See you later!" as they leave. Maintain a positive message.

10.2. Encouraging Open Communication

I've found that by keeping current textbooks and VIN to open with my kids, I learn a lot about them. Kids try to test limits, but they appreciate when parents take time to explain why they've made decisions. Being consistent and open will set the stage for a relationship that can withstand the stress of the teenage years. Additionally, I found that explaining my motto while reinforcing rules and discipline has helped me build bonds with my girls. I've been surprised at how my conversing about rules has helped turn these seemingly negative situations into moments of closeness. Remember, when discussing these topics with your child, be honest—no fibs. A hypervigilant child will never trust if told a flat-out lie is okay. Keep these talks age appropriate; consider the ages given a post as they are my target. Tailor your conversations to your child's needs in order to help her feel safe, understood, and loved.

One of the keys to maintaining strong parent-child relationships with tweens and teens is to stay connected. However, staying connected can be a complicated thing. Sometimes, your kids will wonder why it's important to have a close relationship with you. I've discovered that the more I talk with my kids, the easier it is for them to connect with me at a personal level. They come to me for advice because they trust me to dole out relevant advice that usually doesn't contain any hidden barbs. Positive, beneficial conversations help build your child's trust in you and can head off future problems. Even tough conversations about difficult topics can provide positive experiences—like when your child trusts you with intimate details of their life. This alone can also help head off future problems from peer pressure or the expectations of dating.

10.3. Fostering Independence

12. The Society: The private life decisions of adults often affect society in general. Traditionally, we think of single parents as struggling, destitute, and even morally frail. Their children are often deemed as unruly, unable to behave, academically challenged, delinquent, or worse. There are, of course, some single-parent households in which this is the case, but there are also married parent households in which this is the case. No single-parent home is identical. The problems single parents face often do not come from the fact of their marital status – it's the lack of adequate means to provide for their children. Today's society must redefine the moral norms it has with respect to singleness in parenting roles. It also should clear the remnants of the 'legacy model' which suggests it takes a man and a woman to raise well-balanced children. This is important for single mothers and fathers as well as future generations. A more respectful attitude could lead to more programs designed to aid single-parent homes (i.e. tax reliefs and temporary subsidies), less social stigmatization, and less horizontal segregation. As for the families that do run with the mother or father being at the helm, they serve as a reminder that dual-parent homes might just be a part of human history. A very small part.

11. Fostering Independence. Children who grow up in one-parent homes often develop a strong sense of independence compared to children who grow up in two-parent homes. One explanation could be that due to the number of conflicting messages, a single parent would be unable to nurture a dependent child effectively, and so the child adopts an independent persona to adapt. This brings to mind when a parent remarries the age of the child(ren). If the children are young, the parent is responsible for meeting the child's physical, emotional, and mental needs. If the children are older, the children meet these needs on their own independently, as would their parent be expected to. Presently, there is no evidence-based psychological research that

supports dependency in single-parent homes. Considering that they produce academically high-achieving children, this might give an indication that children raised in single-parent households are no less developed compared to children raised in two-parent homes. People may be monogamous, but that does not mean that humans are inherently psychologically wired to live in a two-parent home.

CHAPTER 11

Self-Development and Growth

In this path, passions, hobbies, meditations, attending groups and courses or continuous professional training can help us. It allows us to take care of ourselves also from a mother or father point of view, instead of getting sucked into the role of caretaker. What do we mean by that? We can explain this concept with an example; give an hour or two of daily routine to do something for ourselves, our talents or personal interests, and you will take care of your children with joy and in a positive way during the rest of the day: the hour for example can be spent learning or performing a sport. But of course, in order to benefit from the advantages related to positive thought, gesture and daily mood, it is necessary to want to change the antiquated various customs we are still taught which are even still in fashion today! Denigrating your physical appearance or professional competence means continuously molding ranking in children's brains, it means transmitting to your children your well-being low level, which in turn is transmitted to you. Listening to your mother's struggles, her weaknesses, makes your child incredibly empathic but also distracted, unable to focus on a proposal or on himself. If, instead, a parent has good self-esteem, security and strength transmitting them to children, children using these good voids will open up to life, to their own discoveries and to the many possibilities which are available to them.

Most parents forget about self-care and learning new things about themselves when they become mothers and fathers. But beyond that, everyone forgets about the human being that dwells inside themselves, that has dreams or needs! It is fundamental to take care of yourself also when you become a mother or a father; it is fundamental to be active in attending developing groups in order to rediscover yourself, take care of your couple, find yourself after having fulfilled the role of father knowing that you can also have fun like when you were single and with reduced responsibilities. It is fundamental to continue your path of self-development and studies even if for work you have to be a full-time caretaker, or try to grow from both a personal perspective and an employment perspective in order to contribute to create a family also from a work type point of view, especially if you are a single parent.

11.1. Pursuing Personal Interests

There are a number of assumptions grown-up children have made about their single parents: that they are invincible; that they are superparents; that they are wholly devoted to them. Let them realize that you need time to relax and set personal targets like any other person and that these commitments they observe make them consider their interests and talents. Once they understand that you have weaknesses and aspirations like any other person, they are steered to establish their life's blueprint and forging ahead to attain their own personal goals. Engage them in discussions about these objectives and ask them about what they have in mind. After school pick-ups, use some of these car moments asking them about their interests instead of discussing household chores and errands. Use the weekends to introduce these activities and specialists who can guide them at suitable tutors. Once adept at their identified area of interest, the positive change in behavior and increased comprehension with their peers and teachers will be real testimony.

The act of self-discovery helps in discovering personal talents and reshaping past ideas of who one is into what you want to become.

Parenting is quite demanding, so setting aside time for revelation and newfound interests will require putting effort into these activities. The benefits of pursuing personal aspirations are a sense of personal fulfillment, satisfaction, and confidence, apart from the talent which can be transformed into a source of additional income or a career change. Involving children in achieving these goals empowers them with the mindset that there are no obstacles to personal fulfillment. Show them how you overcome stumbling blocks on your pursuit for self-discovery and how exciting life becomes when they set their hearts on something.

11.2. Continuing Education

Try to find out how many credits a current student is taking with tuition assistance and CDC subsidy funding. If the Education Center on base cannot offer you assistance, you may be able to transfer your remaining GI Bill benefits to your children as long as they are under 23 but over 18 in college. Check with your base for further information. Also, some states offer college scholarships that are specifically designed to help single parents get a college degree. These grants can help ease the burden of paying for college tuition. Did you previously enroll in a Post Secondary Program and not complete it? Did you know that if you are a young parent, frowned upon by society and your family, discriminated against by educators and seeing no slack cut, that one day you'll lay in bed holding your graduation announcement in your hand thinking, "They frown no more"? School can be a shining light at the end of your parenting struggle. It can leave your children with an indelible impression of how powerful education can be.

Don't underestimate the power and security of an education. Many types of financial and emotional problems have been directly attributed to lack of education. One parent family households take heart from the fact that many scholarships are available for those with an ambition to excel in their studies but facing personal, financial or time constraints. A government program called FASTWEB is a tuition search database that is accessible to single parents. This service hooks into a national database and matches resources with the types of support that are applied for. Please remember that there are significant differences in scholarship opportunities that are solely merit and not need-based as well, so investigate all types of scholarships that might be applicable to you.

11.3. Setting Goals for the Future

You need to think about every single aspect of your life in your planning. Here are some examples of the areas that you might choose to set goals for: relations with your children and their rearing and education, intimate personal relationships, career, home ownership and investments, financial stability, vehicle ownership, health and personal activities, and community involvement. Think about what is most important to you. Select the areas that you would like to concentrate your energy on. Goals for the areas of your life related to your children are particularly important for all single parents. Even if you tend to focus more on your children than yourself, do not just forget about personal goals entirely. It is essential that the children understand the importance of setting goals and achieving them and see that you have interests and ambitions as a person. You should challenge yourself to create good examples for them. By setting goals for yourself, you will be creating an image to them of an individual who is enthusiastic, determined, and hopeful for the future.

As a single parent, what are your aims for the future? You might be finding it difficult to even think about the future while you are dealing with the challenges and duties of everyday life. However, by planning and preparing for the future, you can improve your family's quality of life. Goal setting must be done thoughtfully and meticulously. First, set your long-term goals and then break them down into realistic steps.

Milton Keynes UK
Ingram Content Group UK Ltd.
UKHW030908271124
451618UK00011B/339